RIGHT
STANDING
with
GOD

KENNETH
COPELAND

KENNETH
COPELAND
PUBLICATIONS

Unless otherwise noted, all scripture is from the *King James Version* of the Bible.

Your Right-Standing With God

ISBN 1-57562-120-7   30-0038

10 09 08 07 06 05   10 9 8 7 6 5

© 1983 Eagle Mountain International Church, Incorporated aka
Kenneth Copeland Ministries

Kenneth Copeland Publications
Fort Worth, Texas 76192-0001

For more information about Kenneth Copeland Ministries, call
1-800-600-7395 or visit www.kcm.org.

Your Right-Standing With God

Therefore if any man be in Christ, he is a new creature: old things are passed away; behold, all things are become new. And all things are of God, who hath reconciled us to himself by Jesus Christ, and hath given to us the ministry of reconciliation; To wit, that God was in Christ, reconciling the world unto himself, not imputing their trespasses unto them; and hath committed unto us the word of reconciliation. Now then we are ambassadors for Christ, as though God did

beseech you by us: we pray you in Christ's stead, be ye reconciled to God. For he hath made him to be sin for us, who knew no sin; that we might be made the righteousness of God in him (2 Corinthians 5:17-21).

Any person who is in Christ is a new creature, or a new creation. (The literal Greek says he is a new species of being which never existed before.) He has been **completely recreated.** Old things are passed away, all things are new, and all things are of God—not part of God and part of Satan. Some people think that a man is a schizophrenic when he becomes a Christian—that he has both the nature of God and the nature of Satan—but this is not so. In the new birth, a man's spirit is completely reborn; then it is this man's responsibility to renew his mind to the Word of God and use the Word to take control of his body.

Paul wrote to the believers in Rome, who were born-again, Spirit-filled Christians, and instructed them to renew their minds with the Word (Romans 12:1-2). Their faith was known throughout the world, but they had not learned how to control their minds and bodies with the Word. He wrote to the church at Ephesus along this same line and said, "You have put off the old man and put on the new man, so quit lying and cheating and acting ugly toward one another" (Ephesians 4:24-25). All these people were believers. They had been recreated. They had been made the righteousness of God, **but most of them didn't know it!**

You Are the Righteousness of God

Second Corinthians 5:21 tells us that God made Jesus, Who knew no sin, to be sin for us *"that we might be made the righteousness of God in him."* **As believers in Jesus Christ, we are the righteousness of God Himself!**

What is *righteousness?* It is not a "goody-goody" way of acting or something which can be attained. Righteousness is a free gift of God, provided by Jesus at Calvary through the grace of God. I am not referring to our own righteousness. The Bible says that in the eyes of God *"all our righteousnesses are as filthy rags..."* (Isaiah 64:6). However, we have been given the righteousness of God in Jesus Christ. Through our traditional thinking, we have confused *righteousness* with *holiness*. We think righteousness is the way you act, but this is not true. **Holiness is your conduct—righteousness is what you are.**

The word *righteousness* translated literally means to be "in right-standing." We have been put in right-standing with God. Jesus is the mediator between God and man. When a man accepts Jesus, he moves into a position of new birth. He enters into the kingdom as God's very own child and a joint heir with Jesus Christ. Consequently, there are certain privileges, rights and freedoms that we have as children of God because we are in right-standing with Him.

We didn't get in right-standing with God by being good and acting right. We got there through faith in Jesus Christ and His redemptive work at Calvary. When we accepted the sacrifice of Jesus and made Him the Lord of our lives, then God accepted us. **He had to!** God had already accepted His Son's work on the Cross. He judged it as good, glorified Jesus, and set Him at His own right hand. He called Jesus "God" and inaugurated Him into the highest office in the whole universe. Therefore, the Father is obligated to accept us when we accept Jesus. **Our conduct has absolutely nothing to do with it!**

*"To wit [or to know], that God was in Christ, reconciling the world unto himself, **not imputing their trespasses unto them...**"* (2 Corinthians 5:19). **This verse is saying that God does not hold our sins and trespasses against us.** Very rarely had the whole gospel been preached—only pieces of it! We have heard that God will not forgive a sinner until he confesses his sin, but this is not true. God has

already provided forgiveness and is not holding our trespasses against us.

This teaching about confession of sin stems from 1 John 1:9, *"If we confess our sins, he is faithful and just to forgive us...."* However, this letter was written to Christians for the purpose of their maintaining fellowship with God. The Apostle John wrote in 1 John 2:1-2, *"My little children, these things write I unto you, that ye sin not. And if any man sin, **we** have an advocate with the Father, Jesus Christ the righteous: And he is the propitiation for **our** sins: and not for ours only, but also for the sins of the whole world."* John was referring to the sins of a Christian and was instructing his fellow believers to partake of Jesus' advocate ministry.

John 3:16 says, *"For God so loved the world, that he gave his only begotten Son...."* God loved us and Jesus gave Himself for us while we were in sin. God is not holding our trespasses against us, He is calling us to make Jesus our Lord. He accepted us on the basis of Jesus' right-standing and, in turn, made us in right-standing with Him. The only sin keeping anyone out of the kingdom of God is the sin of rejecting Jesus and what He has provided (John 16:9).

Sin Consciousness

"For the law having a shadow of good things to come, and not the very image of the things, can never with those sacrifices which they offered year by year continually make the comers thereunto perfect" (Hebrews 10:1). Under the Levitical Law, an animal must be offered every 12 months to atone for the sins of the people. The word *atonement* means

"to cover." Actually, this word is not found in the Greek New Testament when it refers to the sacrifice of Jesus. The word which we translate as *atonement* really means "to remit," or to do away with. **These sacrifices could not completely do away with sin, they simply covered them for a year.** The blood of Jesus did not just cover sin, it remitted sin—it did away with sin completely!

With these thoughts in mind, read Hebrews 10:2. *"For then would they not have ceased to be offered? because that the worshippers once purged should have had no more conscience of sins."* If the blood of calves and goats had cleansed them of sin, then they would have had no more conscience of sin, or a sin consciousness. **This sin consciousness produces defeat and a false sense of humility.** It attempts to be humble

11

by defrauding itself and pushing itself back. The Lord did not say, "Deface yourself." He said, "Think of others more highly than you think of yourself." This means that, even when you are standing tall as the righteousness of God, you should elevate your fellow Christian above yourself, making both of you stand tall. When you deface yourself, you make yourself lower than you are. If you asked most Christians, "Are you righteous?" they would say, "Me? No!" They are trying to be humble. They are afraid God wouldn't like it if they said they were righteous. Actually, they are speaking from the way they feel, the way they have been trained, and from ignorance of God's Word.

This type of sin consciousness has caused us to center on and preach sin instead of righteousness. Actually, we have preached a form of condemnation on ourselves. Romans 8:1 says, *"There is therefore now no condemnation to them which are in Christ Jesus."* We have carried "sin tags" with us which are stumbling blocks in the growth of a Christian. Every time we start toward the righteousness of God, Satan will jump up in our path and say, *Remember the ugly things you've done? Don't expect God to forget all that! Who do you think you are? You're too unworthy to approach God!* But the Word says that the blood of Jesus purged our sins—they no longer exist—so we should take the Name of Jesus and drive out this sin consciousness.

The "Sin Tag"

What do I mean by a "sin tag"? A good example is, "Well, I'm just an old sinner saved by grace." No, you

were an old sinner—**you got saved by grace!** Now you are a born-again child of God!

Most everyone is familiar with this scripture, *"For all have sinned, and come short of the glory of God."* This is Romans 3:23 and has been used untold numbers of times in preaching sin; but the Apostle Paul, in writing this letter to the body of believers in Rome, was instructing them about righteousness. Let's read this whole portion of scripture:

> **But now the righteousness of God without the law is manifested, being witnessed by the law and the prophets; Even the righteousness of God which is by faith of Jesus Christ unto all and upon all them that believe: for there is no difference: For all have sinned, and come short of the glory of God; Being**

justified freely by his grace through the redemption that is in Christ Jesus: Whom God hath set forth to be a propitiation through faith in his blood, to declare his righteousness for the remission of sins that are past, through the forbearance of God; To declare, I say, at this time his righteousness: that he might be just, and the justifier of him which believeth in Jesus (Romans 3:21-26).

This is one complete sentence constructed around the righteousness of God. Through this sin consciousness, we have taken out one phrase (the only verse not referring to righteousness) and preached it with no mention of these other verses. Therefore, everyone knows about sin, but no one knows about the righteousness of God. We are well aware of what we have been born out of but have no idea at all of what we have been born into! Colossians 1:12-13 says, *"Giving thanks unto the Father...Who **hath delivered us from** the power of darkness, and **hath translated us into** the kingdom of his dear Son."*

Walk Away From Sin

It is time to believe the Word of God. Did you know that there is no longer a sin problem? Jesus solved it! He stopped the law of sin and death at the Cross and Resurrection. When a person receives salvation, he is put into right-standing with God and recreated by the Spirit of God as if sin had *never* existed! The only problem we have is the sinner problem. It is man's choice. All we need to do is choose righteousness and walk away from the sin problem. It is time to move in line with this. You *were* a sinner—you *have been* forgiven—**you are now His workmanship created in Christ Jesus!** Begin to stand on this instead of your past life. As far as God is concerned, your past life is forgotten. Now *you* need to forget it.

Your past life died the death of the Cross. In Galatians 2:20, the Apostle Paul said it this way: *"I am crucified with Christ: nevertheless I live; yet not I, but Christ liveth in me...."* As I was studying the Word one day, I noticed 2 Corinthians 7:2 where the Apostle Paul was writing to the church at Corinth and said, *"Receive us; we have wronged no man, we have corrupted no man, we have defrauded no man."* When I read this, it startled me, and I said, "Lord, I've caught the Apostle Paul in a lie! I know he wronged and defrauded men. He persecuted the Christians, put them in prison for no legal reason. He stood by and watched as Stephen was stoned to death!" But the Spirit of God spoke to my heart strongly and said, *You watch who you call a liar! The man you are talking about died on the road to Damascus!* You see, Paul could write to Corinth and with a clear conscience, with complete freedom of spirit, say, "I have wronged no man; I have defrauded no man." Paul realized the power of the gospel to raise him up when he was dead in trespasses and sins. He accepted the fact that he was a new creation in Christ Jesus—that his old spirit was dead and gone. His past sins were forgiven and forgotten. Paul was born of God, and the power and force of righteousness was at work in his life.

You are a born-again child of the living God. It's time you began believing in the new birth and what Jesus has provided for you. You will realize that the Father has invited you to come boldly (confidently, without fear) to the throne of grace with your needs and requests. The Bible says that when we pray according to His will, we know He hears us and we know we have the petitions we desired of Him (1 John 5:14-15). **When we pray in the Name of Jesus, we immediately get the ear of God.** First Peter 3:12 says, *"For the eyes of the Lord are over the righteous, and his ears are open unto their prayers..."* and James wrote that *"the effectual fervent prayer of a righteous man availeth much"* (James 5:16).

The following is an example of prayer from this righteousness consciousness:

"Father, I see in Your Word that I have been made the righteousness of God in Jesus Christ. He has provided certain rights for me, and healing is one of these rights. I receive it now in Jesus' Name, and I thank You for it. Your Word also says that You are faithful and just to forgive me of my sins when I confess them, so I take this opportunity to confess this sin and get it out of my life in order to maintain my complete fellowship with You. I receive Your forgiveness now in the Name of Jesus. I may not feel righteous—I may not feel forgiven—but Your Word says it, so it must be true. Satan, I now put on the breastplate of righteousness and come against you with the sword of the Spirit. Healing belongs to me. My body belongs to the God of this universe; I have given it to Him, so in the Name of Jesus Christ of

Nazareth take your sickness and disease and get out!"

You have a *right* to expect your heavenly Father to answer. You have not prayed in your name; you have prayed in Jesus' Name. **His righteousness (right-standing with God) is yours!** A righteousness consciousness expects God's Word to be true and plans for success.

This kind of prayer is tough in the world of the spirit, and it will bring results in the physical world. After you have prayed to God and taken authority over Satan, you should take authority over your physical body. Speak to it in the Name of Jesus and command it to conform to the Word of God that says it is healed by the stripes of Jesus. I have done this and had my body to shape up immediately. You see, **the world of the spirit controls the world of the natural.** A Spirit created all matter—His name is Almighty God, and He is our Father! The righteousness of God is what it's all about!

Conformity With God

We have discussed the fact that Jesus was aware of His rights—His righteousness—with God. He relied on it completely during His earthly ministry and ministered freely in any way He chose. He did what the Father told Him to do. This is the key to the mystery: The Father was in Jesus and Jesus was in the Father— *they were one.* The will of Jesus conformed completely to the will of God. They walked together and worked together in total harmony. **This is how believers are to live with God**—not His will deforming ours or our will bucking against His, but both wills conformed together.

Conformity with God is a much higher form of life than just merely being in submission to Him. When you conform to God, when you conform to His will and do His work, you will reach a point where you will lean entirely on your right-standing with Him. Then you, like Jesus, will not hesitate to lay hands on the sick and expect God to heal them. You will freely exercise your rights in the kingdom of God as His child and as a joint heir with Jesus. God sees you through the blood of the Lamb, and He sees you the same as He sees Jesus. This is almost more than the human mind can conceive, but it's true! I will prove it to you from the prayers of Jesus Himself. Jesus knew how to pray, and if anyone on earth could get his prayers answered, Jesus could. Therefore, it would be to our advantage to examine some of the things He prayed.

In John 17:20-21, Jesus is praying to God at a vital time in His earthly ministry. It is just moments before Calvary, and He says, *"Neither pray I for these alone [His disciples], but for them also which shall believe on me through their word."* This includes you and me because each of us received Jesus, either directly or indirectly, through the words of one or more of these men.

So Jesus is referring to us and prays, *"That they all may be one; **as thou, Father, art in me, and I in thee."** Here* is the example we are to follow in being one with each other, in conforming to one another and in conforming to Jesus. We are to be one with the Father as Jesus was one with Him. First Corinthians 6:17 says, *"But he that is joined unto the Lord is one spirit."* Another translation says, *"He that is joined unto the Lord is one* *spirit with Him."* The Holy Spirit is the life force of God, and He lives in the heart of a believer. We get our life from Him. As Jesus taught in John 15:5, He is the vine and we are the branches. **Praise the Lord!**

When you begin to operate in these things, when you begin to act on the righteousness which Jesus has given you, then you will realize that many of the differences which have separated the Body of Christ for years are actually foolish and unimportant. **We have bickered and fought with one another over the most ridiculous issues.**

"Father," Jesus prayed in John 17:23, "show them that You love them as much as You love Me." God loves you *as much* as His own Son! He sees you as equal with Jesus—there is no difference in His eyes. Begin to see yourself as God sees you and take advantage of His free gift of righteousness. **Your right-standing with God was bought with a high price...don't take it lightly.**

Prayer for Salvation and
Baptism in the Holy Spirit

Heavenly Father, I come to You in the Name of Jesus. Your Word says, "Whosoever shall call on the name of the Lord shall be saved" (Acts 2:21). I am calling on You. I pray and ask Jesus to come into my heart and be Lord over my life according to Romans 10:9-10: "If thou shalt confess with thy mouth the Lord Jesus, and shalt believe in thine heart that God hath raised him from the dead, thou shalt be saved. For with the heart man believeth unto righteousness; and with the mouth confession is made unto salvation." I do that now. I confess that Jesus is Lord, and I believe in my heart that God raised Him from the dead.

I am now reborn! I am a Christian—a child of Almighty God! I am saved! You also said in Your Word, "If ye then, being evil, know how to give good gifts unto your children: HOW MUCH MORE shall your heavenly Father give the Holy Spirit to them that ask him?" (Luke 11:13). I'm also asking You to fill me with the Holy Spirit. Holy Spirit, rise up within me as I praise

God. I fully expect to speak with other tongues as You give me the utterance (Acts 2:4). In Jesus' Name. Amen!

Begin to praise God for filling you with the Holy Spirit. Speak those words and syllables you receive—not in your own language, but the language given to you by the Holy Spirit. You have to use your own voice. God will not force you to speak. Don't be concerned with how it sounds. It is a heavenly language!

Continue with the blessing God has given you and pray in the spirit every day.

You are a born-again, Spirit-filled believer. You'll never be the same!

Find a good church that boldly preaches God's Word and obeys it. Become a part of a church family who will love and care for you as you love and care for them.

We need to be connected to each other. It increases our strength in God. It's God's plan for us.

Make it a habit to watch the *Believer's Voice of Victory* television broadcast and become a doer of the Word, who is blessed in his doing (James 1:22-25).

About the Author

Kenneth Copeland is co-founder and president of Kenneth Copeland Ministries in Fort Worth, Texas, and best-selling author of books that include *Managing God's Mutual Funds—Yours and His, How to Discipline Your Flesh* and *Honor—Walking in Honesty, Truth and Integrity*.

Now in his 35th year as a minister of the gospel of Christ and teacher of God's Word, Kenneth is the recording artist of such award-winning albums as his Grammy nominated *Only the Redeemed, In His Presence, He Is Jehovah* and his most recently released *Just a Closer Walk*. He also co-stars as the character Wichita Slim in the children's adventure videos *The Gunslinger, Covenant Rider* and the movie *The Treasure of Eagle Mountain*, and as Daniel Lyon in the *Commander Kellie and the Superkids*_{SM} videos *Armor of Light* and *Judgment: The Trial of Commander Kellie*.

With the help of offices and staff in the United States, Canada, England, Australia, South Africa and Ukraine, Kenneth is fulfilling his vision to boldly preach the uncompromised Word of God from the top of this world, to the bottom, and all the way around. His ministry reaches millions of people worldwide through daily and Sunday TV broadcasts, magazines, teaching tapes and videos, conventions and campaigns, and the World Wide Web.

Learn more about
Kenneth Copeland Ministries
by visiting our Web site
at **www.kcm.org**

Books Available From
Kenneth Copeland Ministries

by Kenneth Copeland

* A Ceremony of Marriage
  A Matter of Choice
  Covenant of Blood
  Faith and Patience—The Power Twins
* Freedom From Fear
  Giving and Receiving
  Honor—Walking in Honesty, Truth and Integrity
  How to Conquer Strife
  How to Discipline Your Flesh
  How to Receive Communion
  In Love There Is No Fear
  Know Your Enemy
  Living at the End of Time—A Time of Supernatural Increase
  Love Never Fails
  Managing God's Mutual Funds—Yours and His
  Mercy—The Divine Rescue of the Human Race
* Now Are We in Christ Jesus
  One Nation Under God (gift book with CD enclosed)
* Our Covenant With God
  Partnership, Sharing the Vision—Sharing the Grace
* Prayer—Your Foundation for Success
* Prosperity: The Choice Is Yours
  Rumors of War
* Sensitivity of Heart
* Six Steps to Excellence in Ministry
* Sorrow Not! Winning Over Grief and Sorrow
* The Decision Is Yours
* The Force of Faith
* The Force of Righteousness
  The Image of God in You
  The Laws of Prosperity
* The Mercy of God (Available in Spanish only)

The Secret Place of God's Protection (gift book with CD enclosed)
The Unbeatable Spirit of Faith
* Walk in the Spirit (Available in Spanish only)
Walk With God
Well Worth the Wait
Words That Heal (gift book with CD enclosed)
Your Promise of Protection—The Power of the 91st Psalm

Books Co-Authored by Kenneth and Gloria Copeland
Family Promises
Healing Promises
Prosperity Promises
Protection Promises

* From Faith to Faith—A Daily Guide to Victory
From Faith to Faith—A Perpetual Calendar

One Word From God Series
• One Word From God Can Change Your Destiny
• One Word From God Can Change Your Family
• One Word From God Can Change Your Finances
• One Word From God Can Change Your Formula for Success
• One Word From God Can Change Your Health
• One Word From God Can Change Your Nation
• One Word From God Can Change Your Prayer Life
• One Word From God Can Change Your Relationships

Over The Edge—A Youth Devotional
Load Up—A Youth Devotional
Pursuit of His Presence—A Daily Devotional
Pursuit of His Presence—A Perpetual Calendar

Other Books Published by KCP
The First 30 Years—A Journey of Faith
    The story of the lives of Kenneth and Gloria Copeland.
Real People. Real Needs. Real Victories.
    A book of testimonies to encourage your faith.

*Available in Spanish

John G. Lake—His Life, His Sermons, His Boldness of Faith
The Holiest of All by Andrew Murray
The New Testament in Modern Speech by
    Richard Francis Weymouth
Unchained by Mac Gober

Products Designed for Today's Children and Youth

And Jesus Healed Them All (confession book and CD gift package)
Baby Praise Board Book
Baby Praise Christmas Board Book
Noah's Ark Coloring Book
The Best of *Shout!* Adventure Comics
The *Shout!* Giant Flip Coloring Book
The *Shout!* Joke Book
The *Shout!* Super-Activity Book
Wichita Slim's Campfire Stories

*Commander Kellie and the Superkids*_{SM} Books:

The SWORD Adventure Book
*Commander Kellie and the Superkids*_{SM} Solve-It-
    Yourself Mysteries
*Commander Kellie and the Superkids*_{SM} Adventure Series
    Middle Grade Novels by Christopher P.N. Maselli
        #1 The Mysterious Presence
        #2 The Quest for the Second Half
        #3 Escape From Jungle Island
        #4 In Pursuit of the Enemy
        #5 Caged Rivalry
        #6 Mystery of the Missing Junk
        #7 Out of Breath
        #8 The Year Mashela Stole Christmas

World Offices of
Kenneth Copeland Ministries

For more information about KCM and a free
catalog, please write the office nearest you:

Kenneth Copeland Ministries
Fort Worth, Texas 76192-0001

Kenneth Copeland
Locked Bag 2600
Mansfield Delivery Centre
QUEENSLAND 4122
AUSTRALIA

Kenneth Copeland
Post Office Box 15
BATH
BA1 3XN
U.K.

Kenneth Copeland
Private Bag X 909
FONTAINEBLEAU
2032
REPUBLIC OF
SOUTH AFRICA

Kenneth Copeland
Post Office Box 378
Surrey, B.C.
V3T 5B6
CANADA

Kenneth Copeland Ministries
Post Office Box 84
L'VIV 79000
UKRAINE

Believer's Voice of Victory Television Broadcast

Join Kenneth and Gloria Copeland and the *Believer's Voice of Victory* broadcasts Monday through Friday and on Sunday each week, and learn how faith in God's Word can take your life from ordinary to extraordinary. This teaching from God's Word is designed to get you where you want to be—*on top!*

You can catch the *Believer's Voice of Victory* broadcast on your local, cable or satellite channels.

*Check your local listings for times and stations in your area.

Believer's Voice of Victory Magazine

Enjoy inspired teaching and encouragement from Kenneth and Gloria Copeland and guest ministers each month in the *Believer's Voice of Victory* magazine. Also included are real-life testimonies of God's miraculous power and divine intervention in the lives of people just like you!

It's more than just a magazine—it's a ministry.

To receive a FREE subscription to *Believer's Voice of Victory,* write to:

Kenneth Copeland Ministries
Fort Worth, Texas 76192-0001

Or call: 1-800-600-7395   (7 a.m.-5 p.m. CT)
Or visit our Web site at: **www.kcm.org**

If you are writing from outside the U.S., please contact the KCM office nearest you. Addresses for all Kenneth Copeland Ministries offices are listed on the previous pages.